Bird Garden
COLOUR ME
COLLECTION

LEGAL

AKNOWLEDGEMENTS

I would like to thank my incredible team of colourists who creatively colour and test out the illustrations before publication. The book would not be possible without you and thank you also for your wonderful support of me as an artist and for your colouring talent which continues to amaze me. You are truly inspirational to the colouring world. xxx

FRONT COVER

"Feathered Friends" page coloured by Lesley Smitheringale
"Peacock" card and matching envelope coloured by Lesley Smitheringale

BACK COVER

"Garden Bouquet" coloured by Millie Plastaras
"Chatter at the Feeding Tray" coloured by Kelly Darling
"Birds of a Feather Bookmarks" and "Hummingingbirds & Fuchsias" coloured by Erna Piatek

Bird Garden
COLOUR ME
COLLECTION

ABOUT THE ARTIST

Lesley lives and works in her home studio in the Redlands area of Queensland, Australia. She was born in Glasgow, Scotland where she obtained a BA with Honours in Design at Glasgow School of Art. She then did further training to become an art teacher and after teaching for twenty years to Middle and High School students, Lesley took the plunge and decided to work for herself. She currently teaches extra-curricular art to children, produces her own artwork, hand-made gifts, illustrates and self-publishes art & craft books.

KEEP UP-TO-DATE

If you love to colour and tangle, Lesley also runs a website and online Shop at Colouring and Tangling where she offers inspiration, tips & techniques, video instruction and a large range of products such as books, printable pdfs, Calendars, Cards, Bookmarks, Artist Prints and Giftware for colourists and lovers of zentangle-inspired art. Why not visit and sign up for Lesley's Newsletter and keep up-to-date.

Lesley also hosts a private Facebook Group which fans and colourists of her illustrations can join, offering you the opportunity to showcase your colourings from any of her books and products, meet a creative, virtual community and enjoy giveaways, video instruction and up-to-date news of new colouring resource s.

Visit https://www.facebook.com/groups/LesleySmitheringaleArtColouring/ and ask to join!

http://www.colouringandtangling.com
http://www.colouringandtangling.com/shop
https://www.facebook.com/colouringandtangling
https://www.etsy.com/shop/ColouringandTangling

7 THEMED GIFT PACKS

Bird & Garden
COLOUR ME
COLLECTION

Containing:
Page
Rectangle Bookmarks
Corner Heart Bookmarks
Gift Bag Template
Tags
Cards
Matching Envelope Template

Feathered Friends
{parrots, irises, chrysanthemums,
crocuses, hibiscus, Monarch butterfly}

Chrysanthemum & Bumble Bee

Chatter at the Feeding Tray
{Tulips & British Birds: l to r golden finches x 2,
blue tit and spotted woodpecker}

Garden Bouquet
{Hummingbird, roses, pansies,
magnolias, foxgloves, daisies}

Hummingbirds & Fuchsias

Peacock

Watering the Garden
{Sunflowers, chickens & field mouse}

Gift bags and tags

The cards, matching envelopes and gift bag templates are very easy to assemble.
Simpy colour, fold along the lines & glue the tabs to assemble.
The gift bag can be completely closed by glueing one top flap on top of the other, or punch a hole in both top flaps and tie together with pretty ribbon or cord.

Pop whatever you wish inside the box such as lollies, baked treats, or small gifts.

TIP: Scan your coloured flat template before assembling so that you can make lots more

The Love that comes from a Mother's Heart lives in the hearts of her children forever

The love that comes from a Mother's Heart lives in the hearts of her children forever

A Mother holds her child's hand for a short while and their heart forever

Corner Heart Bookmarks

Feathered Friends

1. Colour the hearts
2. Cut out
3. Fold in half and along the tab
4. Glue tab and tuck inside the heart
5. Slide over the corner of a page

Feathered Friends
Gift Bag

Bird Garden
COLOUR ME
COLLECTION

Feathered Friends
Gift Bag for Mum

Bird
Garden
COLOUR ME
COLLECTION

The Love that comes from a Mother's Heart lives in the hearts of her children forever

Feathered Friends
Tags

Bird Garden
COLOUR ME
COLLECTION

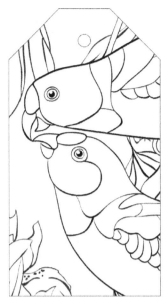

The love that comes from a Mother's Heart lives in the hearts of her children forever

A Mother holds her child's hand for a short while and their heart forever

Feathered Friends

www.colouringandtangling.com

Feathered Friends

www.colouringandtangling.com

Feathered Friends
Envelope

Bird & Garden
COLOUR ME
COLLECTION

To:

From:

www.colouringandtangling.com

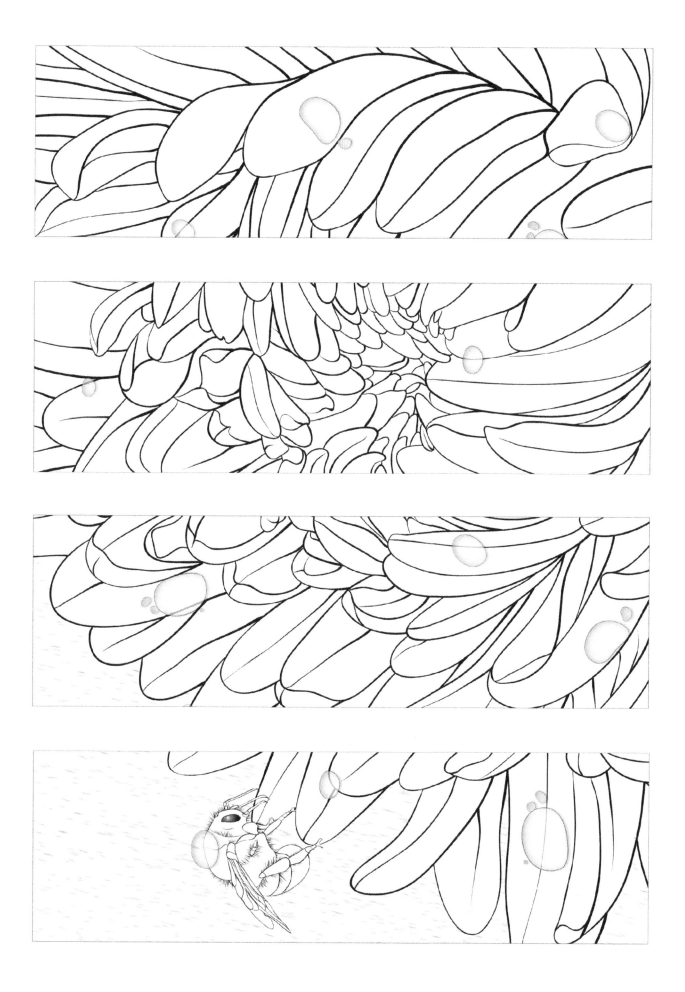

Corner Heart Bookmarks
Chrysanthemum & Bumble Bee

1. Colour the hearts
2. Cut out
3. Fold in half and along the tab
4. Glue tab and tuck inside the heart
5. Slide over the corner of a page

Chrysanthemum
& Bumble Bee
Gift Bag

Bird Garden
COLOUR ME
COLLECTION

Chrysanthemum & Bumble Bee Tags

Bird & Garden
COLOUR ME
COLLECTION

Chrysanthemum & Bumble Bee

www.colouringandtangling.com

Chrysanthemum & Bumble Bee

www.colouringandtangling.com

Chrysanthemum
& Bumble Bee
Envelope

To:

From:

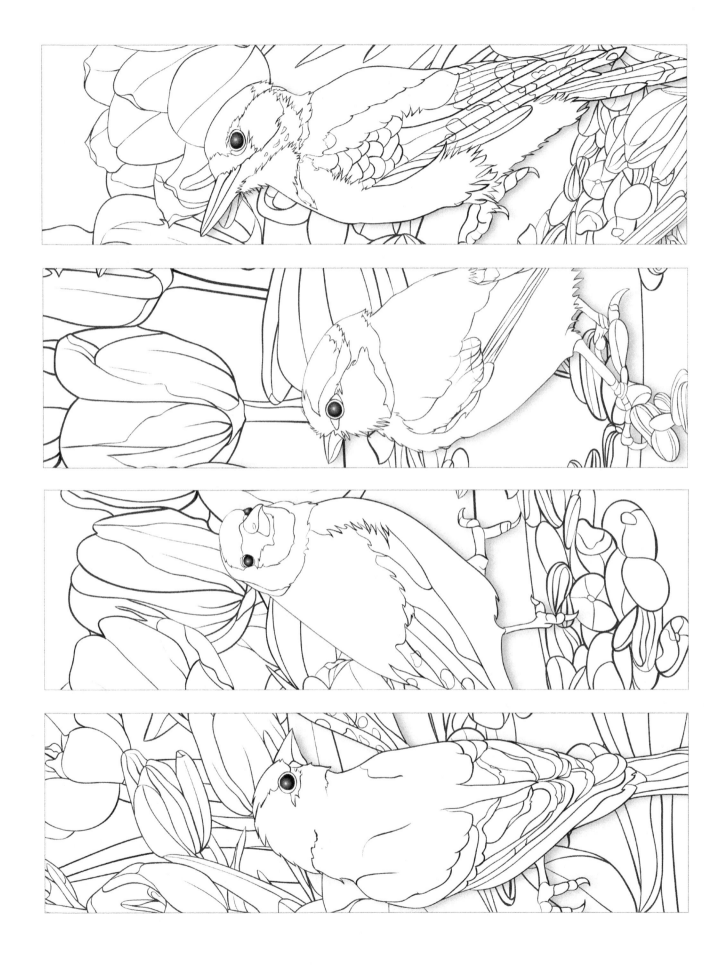

Bird Garden
COLOUR ME
COLLECTION

Corner Heart Bookmarks
Chatter at the Feeding Tray

1. Colour the hearts
2. Cut out
3. Fold in half and along the tab
4. Glue tab and tuck inside the heart
5. Slide over the corner of a page

Chatter at the Feeding Tray Gift Bag

Chatter at the Feeding Tray
Tags

Bird
Garden
COLOUR ME
COLLECTION

Chatter at the Feeding Tray

Chatter at the Feeding Tray

Chatter at the
Feeding Tray
Envelope

Bird
Garden
COLOUR ME
COLLECTION

To:

From:

www.colouringandtangling.com

Garden Bouquet Gift Bag

Garden Bouquet

Garden Bouquet

www.colouringandtangling.com

Garden Bouquet

www.colouringandtangling.com

Garden Bouquet
Envelope

To:

From:

www.colouringandtangling.com

COLOUR ME COLLECTION

Corner Heart Bookmarks
Hummingbirds & Fuchsias

1. Colour the hearts
2. Cut out
3. Fold in half and along the tab
4. Glue tab and tuck inside the heart
5. Slide over the corner of a page

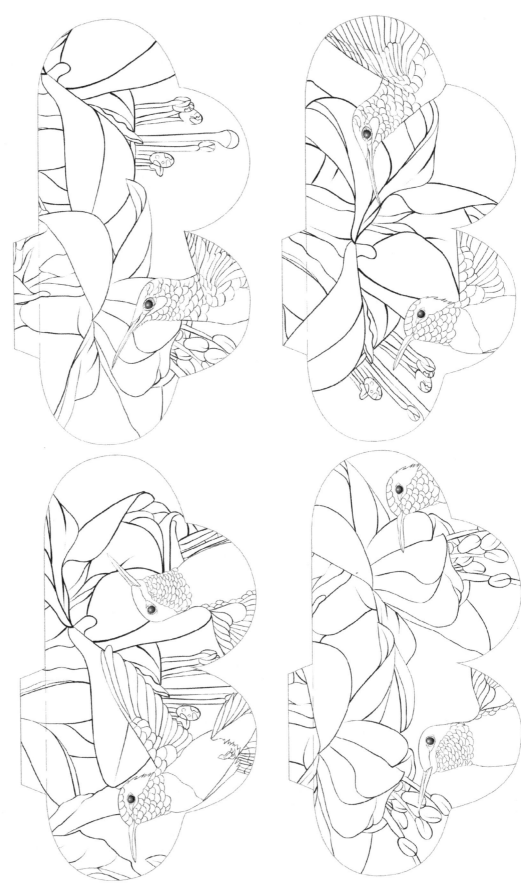

Hummingbirds & Fuchsias Gift Bag

Hummingbird &
Fuchsias Tags

COLOUR ME
COLLECTION

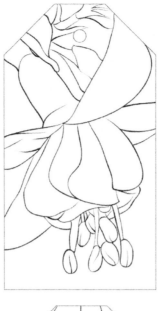

Hummingbirds & Fuchsias

www.colouringandtangling.com

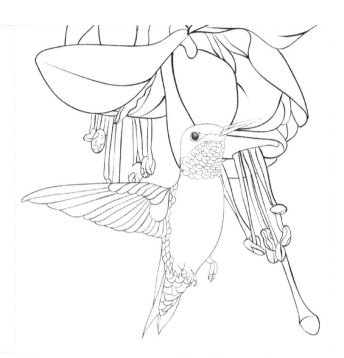

Hummingbirds & Fuchsias

www.colouringandtangling.com

Hummingbirds
& Fuchsias
Envelope

Bird
Garden
COLOUR ME
COLLECTION

To:

From:

www.colouringandtangling.com

COLOURING
and
TANGLING

Peacock Corner Heart Bookmarks

Peacock
Gift Bag

Bird
Garden
COLOUR ME
COLLECTION

Peacock Tags

Peaccock

www.colouringandtangling.com

Peaccock

www.colouringandtangling.com

Peacock
Envelope

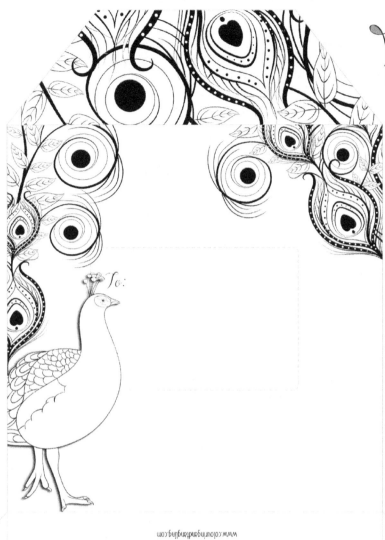

To:

www.colouringandtangling.com

From:

Corner Heart Bookmarks
Watering the Garden

1. Colour the hearts
2. Cut out
3. Fold in half and along the tab
4. Give tab and tuck inside the heart
5. Slide over the corner of a page

Watering the Garden
Gift Bag

Watering the Garden
Tags

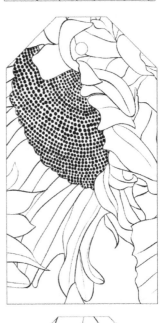

Watering the Garden

www.colouringandtangling.com

Watering the Garden

www.colouringandtangling.com

Watering the
Garden
Envelope

To:

www.colouringandtangling.com

From:

HAVE YOU SEEN LESLEY'S OTHER BOOKS?

   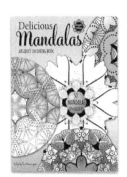

ON AMAZON AND PDF
& SPIRAL BOUND ARTIST EDITIONS

Check out Lesley's other colouring books which are available as:
* budget books on Amazon
* spiral-bound artist editions printed onto 200gsm card stock
(mailed out from Australia)
* instant download PDF so you can print out at home onto your
favourite paper or take the file to a print lab or office supplies
outlet to have printed and bound into your very own book.

LINKS

https://amazon.com/author/lesleysmitheringale
http://www.colouringandtangling.com
http://www.colouringandtangling.com/shop
https://www.etsy.com/shop/ColouringandTangling

Made in the USA
Columbia, SC
06 December 2021

50544982R00065